Quick and Fun Learning Activities for Babies

Ina Massler Levin, M.A. &
Michael H. Levin, M.A.

Teacher Created Materials, Inc.

SAg 00-640 ChildCare May 2000 $8.95

Cover Design by Larry Bauer

Made in U.S.A.
ISBN 1-55734-553-8

Order Number TCM 553

Table of Contents

Introduction

Babies. Cute, cuddly, adorable. Cranky, crabby, ornery. Which words describe your baby? Depending on the moment—probably any one of them!

Babies are such delights in our lives. Just the thought of them conjures pictures of smiling faces, huge yawns, glorious gurgles, and clapping hands. Babies also bring to mind endless diapers and seemingly endless nights. But mostly babies make us think of fun, for babies are wonderful playmates.

From the minute your baby starts to wiggle in her bassinet and until the day her crib can no longer contain her, she will bring you countless hours of sheer, unadulterated joy. Babies were made to play. And while playing, your baby will be learning.

We did lots of things which were fun-filled, quick, and easy. We took lots of trips. We created presents for others. Many of our early toys were homemade. Our house was generally messy, but our babies were happy and so were we. We understand you really want to play with baby all day, but the reality is that there is dinner to be cooked, a house to clean, an occupation or two, and the whole host of other responsibilities to be attended to. How well we remembered all of this as we were writing this book.

In realizing that so much has to be done, the activities you find here are geared to families that lead busy lives. The games and outings we suggest will take little preparation and cleanup. Both you and your baby will benefit, not only from the interaction these activities are designed to achieve but also from the closeness you will derive.

Our age designation is divided between "younger baby" and "older baby." A young baby is anywhere from birth to about 4–5 months, and older babies are from about 5–12 months. However, as the parent, you know best which activities are developmentally appropriate and match the stage of development your baby is in at the time. For instance, if an activity says to roll a ball to your baby and your baby doesn't try to pick it up, don't despair. He probably isn't ready for it. Try again in a week or a month. When he is ready, and only when he is ready, will he attempt to do something. As hard as it is for parents not to push, forcing activities won't get you anywhere with your baby. When your child is ready to crawl, sit, or talk, he will. Babies work on their own timetables, not ours.

However, their timetables make us appreciate them all the more. When our expectations are temporarily forgotten, we can see the world through their eyes. You may find that as your baby learns to play, her activity will reawaken your ability to play, too. Have fun, both of you!

Safety Concerns

Where your baby is concerned, safety is of the utmost importance. The activities in this book have been designed with that in mind. If there are special concerns for a particular activity, it is noted in the description of the activity. The statistics from the U.S. Bureau of Maternal and Child Health say that every month nearly 400 children under four years old die in the United States due to accidents. The truly sad part is that most of these accidents could have been prevented. Using safety precautions with babies is not an option; it's a must. Keep in mind the following about your baby.

◆ As soon as your baby can wiggle, he can fall. Never leave your baby unattended on a changing table, a couch, a bed, or any other place he can fall from.

◆ Once your baby starts crawling, close doors to rooms he shouldn't be in. Use gates on stairs. Babies wave their arms and legs. By three months he may be able to grab onto things. Keep out of his reach anything that has the slightest potential for harm. A mug of hot coffee in your hand or a potted plant he can reach and tip are examples.

◆ Little ones are curious about everything and put just about anything in their mouths. Never leave him alone with anything that shouldn't be in his mouth. This means you will need to supervise him carefully. If you see him picking up a rock or seashell, you will need to take it from him before it can do harm. Check out his toys. If the box says for three and up, for instance, it may have to do with the size of the toy parts, rather than whether or not the child will find it fun. When our children were babies, our own rule of thumb was to never give them anything that wasn't about the size of our fists.

◆ Babies love to play in the water. Water play takes constant supervision. If the phone rings while you're bathing your baby, just let it ring. The caller will call another time. No call is as important as your baby's safety.

◆ Safety straps should be used. Of course, you always buckle your baby's car seat (and yours), but there are many others to buckle—those on changing tables, baby carriers, baby backpacks, strollers, high chairs, and shopping carts. However, just strapping your baby in does not give you permission to leave him alone. Your supervision here will need to be as rigorous as any other time. When it comes to safety, we cannot be too careful. Your baby will start to creep somewhere around the seventh month and crawl around eight months. Before this happens, take a crawling trip around your house. Get down on your hands and knees and check out the safety factor in your house. This is a good activity in which to involve siblings because they often see things that adults might not. Are there plugs that need capping or cords that need to be moved? Are there knickknacks on a shelf that could cause harm? Spend some time correcting this situation before baby even discovers it. Take the time now to be safe so you can enjoy your baby.

Stuff Around the House

For the most part, when you play with your baby, you will not need any "stuff" other than yourself and child to play with. However, it is a good idea to collect any stuff you may need before you begin any activity. If nothing else, having materials centrally located will make your life a little easier. This will be one less thing you need to think about while tending to your baby.

Collect the materials as you can. Find a central location to dump them in. We found a laundry basket the best for storing this kind of hodgepodge. It was lightweight, could hold a lot, and had handles for easy transport.

Do not feel that you have to have every item on the list in your collection. We have purposely not specified that you have two pots or three spoons, for only you can determine what is right for you. Even this will change as your baby grows.

Although there are activities throughout this book that employ these materials, don't feel you must use them only in the way they are described. As a matter of fact, throw this book onto the top of the basket. Then, when the mood strikes, play, improvise, and, above all, have fun with your baby.

Stuff to Have Around the House

- Blanket
- Beach towel
- Pots and pans (with fitting lids)
- Wooden spoons (various sizes)
- Metal spoons (teaspoon, tablespoon)
- Balls (beach ball, tennis ball, large and small balls)
- Tin foil
- Boxes of various sizes
- Laundry basket
- Mirrors (nonbreakable)
- Books (all kinds)
- Tape recorder
- Radio
- CD player
- Tapes and CDs (all kinds)
- Paper towel and toilet paper tubes
- Wrapping paper
- Clean, white athletic socks
- Marker
- Hats
- Plastic cups
- Bubbles and wand (tightly capped)
- Bowls of various sizes (nonbreakable)
- Empty, hinged diaper wipe box
- Handkerchief
- Blocks
- Rattles
- Fabric squares
- Pull toy
- Bells
- Safe stuffed animals (no detachable parts)

The First Year

The first year of a baby's life is marked with tremendous growth. Below are some of the milestones of that year and an approximate time that these may take place. It is extremely important to remember that each baby develops at his or her individual pace.

Birth to Six Weeks

In the first month, babies may:

be sleepy.

begin to recognize mother.

begin to listen to human voices, especially the high tones.

have little control of the body.

startle at sharp sounds.

Six Weeks to Three Months

Babies may:

show a real interest in the world.

become stronger and more coordinated.

watch their hands.

begin to smile.

enjoy looking at human faces.

begin tracking objects.

Three Months to Five-and-One-Half Months

Babies may:

respond to new voices.

finger objects with both hands.

bring objects to the mouth.

enjoy kicking against things.

gain good head control in an upright position.

learn to reach.

become sensitive to words, sounds, and voices.

differentiate self from image in mirror.

laugh out loud.

Five-and-One-Half Months to Eight Months

Babies may:

turn over well and try to sit up.

spend more time in an upright position.

shy away from strangers.

become very curious about surroundings.

begin to clap hands.

try to crawl.

bat at objects.

start to problem solve.

Eight Months to Twelve Months

Babies may:

crawl well/may begin to try walking.

begin to understand language.

develop fine motor skills.

explore everything.

try to imitate and mimic.

Table of Contents for Music and Movement

Music and Movement Introduction

"Lullaby and goodnight, go to sleep now sleep tight" begins the classic lullaby. Rocking your baby and crooning a tune give vivid reminders of what babies are all about. What a golden opportunity parents are afforded when they sing their little one to sleep. But music can be more than lullabies. It can be loud marching music or rock and roll. It can be the inspiration for an impromptu dance or song. The rhythm from the music may make your baby turn his head in curious fascination as if to say, "Where is that coming from?" We live in an age where music is readily available. You can turn on the radio or put on a tape or a CD and have instantaneous music. Expose your baby early in his life to all types of music. Sing to him often. Even if you think you don't have a wonderful voice, your baby will think it is lyrical. Hold him, and hum and sway with him. He'll like the movement and the music together. Soon he'll be humming some of the melodies back to you.

A baby tape recorder is a good investment to make early on in your baby's life. Of course, you can use one that you have, but a small tape player especially made for young children will be easier for you to transport. It is also less likely to break when it falls.

Begin a tape collection for your baby early on. A suggested list of tapes and CDs for babies can be found on page 78.

Listen to children's songs and learn them. By the time your baby is speaking, he may attempt to sing them with you.

Music and movement often go together, but some of the activities in this section are simply movement. Movement, as we define it, is getting baby to move often in a way that he might not do on his own. For instance, a little baby can't yet move his legs in a bicycle movement, but you can do this as you are getting him dressed. Add movement to your daily routine, especially if you have a very active baby. Movement can make changing time much easier.

Music and Movement

Favorite Lullabies

Baby can still be sung to sleep when you're not there.

Materials

Tape recorder
Blank tapes
Music and/or words to
 lullabies

Activity

Sing lots of lullabies to your baby before she goes to sleep at night. Take note of the ones she likes the best. (If you need to learn some lullabies, take a trip to a children's book and music store. Look through the tapes and choose one.) As you sing to baby, turn the tape recorder on and tape yourself singing. Play back the tape and check that it indeed recorded. Add to the tape at various times. When you need a break, or your baby needs some soothing, pop the tape into the recorder and play a medley of your baby's favorites.

Motor Boat

Materials

Words to the poem
 (See below.)

Activity

Pick up your baby securely in your arms. As you say the words, move in a circle, holding baby. When the motor boat says to go slow, just move slowly in a circle. As the motor boat starts to go fast, go faster. When you are told to "step on the gas," speed up your movement. Once your baby is walking, hold both his hands and walk in a circle with him at the speed you indicate. Be careful so that neither you nor the baby become dizzy.

Motor Boat
Motor boat, motor boat,
Go so slow.
Motor boat, motor boat,
Go so fast,
Motor boat, motor boat,
Step on the gas.

Music and Movement

Playing an Instrument

Dust off your banjo and entertain your baby.

Materials

Musical instrument

Activity

Your baby is too young to play an instrument, but you aren't. Dust off your guitar, wipe off your harmonica, or get a new kazoo. Then, place your baby near your instrument, either lying on a blanket, in a baby carrier, or on a chair. With your baby settled comfortably nearby, play your instrument for him. Depending on his mood and your skill level, you can vary the type of music you choose to play. As your baby gets older, let him touch the instrument. Let him feel the vibrating guitar strings or try to cover the holes on the recorder.

A Music Box

Materials

Music box

Activity

When you are asked what gift you might like for your baby, request a music box that plays a lullaby. Place the music box in baby's room where she can hear it. Since music boxes are fragile, it would be wise to put it well out of her reach. When you put her down for a nap or to bed at night, tell her you are going to do something very special for her. Then, turn on the music box and let her listen. (As she gets older, you may want to show her the music box and even let her touch it, but remember for safety's sake that this is not a baby toy and needs close supervision.)

Music and Movement

Jack and Jill

Activity

Sit in a chair. Place your baby on your knee, holding her comfortably under the arms. Recite the words to the nursery rhyme "Jack and Jill" one time through to get the rhythm. Now say the nursery rhyme again. This time as you say, "up the hill," gently lift your baby into the air. When you say, "Jack fell down," gently lower your baby onto your knee. As you say, "And Jill came tumbling after," gently rock your baby on your knee. For variation place your baby on your right knee and then your left knee. (The lesser known second verse is included. Try making up your own movements for these lines.)

Materials

Words for Jack and Jill (See below.)

"Jack and Jill"

(Traditional Nursery Rhyme)

Jack and Jill went up the hill,

To fetch a pail of water,

Jack fell down and broke his crown,

And Jill came tumbling after.

And up Jack got and home did trot

As fast as he could caper,

To old Dame Dobb who fixed his nob

With vinegar and brown paper.

Music and Movement

Enjoying Music

Hum along if the music moves you!

Materials
Music (records, tapes, radio, even singing)

Activity
Turn some music on. Any music that you enjoy will do. Gently lift your baby in your arms. Start swaying to the music and tell your baby you are about to dance. Start moving around, dancing with your baby in your arms. This can be a great family activity. As everyone dances in a circle, you stand in the middle and dance around with baby in your arms.

Where Are the Bells?

Materials
Large bells (The commercially prepared ones, secured to plastic straps, are the safest.)
Blanket

Activity
Place your baby on the blanket. Do not show him the bells. Gently shake the bells next to the his left ear. When he turns his head, shake them near the right ear. Do it a few more times and then let him shake the bells. With older babies, have them sit up and shake the bells above their heads as well as near their ears. (**Note:** Before you know it, the time will probably come when your baby will probably want to shake the bells himself. Make sure that they are secured to the plastic, too big for him to choke on, and not so heavy that he hits himself in the head. Then, let him make his own music.)

Music and Movement

Are You Sleeping?

Baby won't be asleep when you do this with her.

Materials
*Large bells
(The commercially
prepared ones,
secured to plastic
straps, are the
safest.)*

Activity
Using a set of jingle bells, or any other bell, sing the song, "Are You Sleeping?" to your baby. You can hold your baby, or she can be lying down. At the last line, "Ding ding dong, ding ding dong," ring the bell at each word. As your baby gets older, let her try to ring the bell.

Classical Music

Let baby hear various types of music.

Materials
*Radio tuned to a
classical radio
station
CDs of classical
music*

Activity
Take a moment to determine the radio station in your area that plays classical music. Then, give your baby an opportunity to listen to it. Place a radio turned to classical music near your baby. If you have a collection of classical CDs, this is the time to play them. She can listen to the music as she plays, or as she drifts off to sleep. Ours often fell asleep for their afternoon naps to the strains of Brahms or Mozart.

Music and Movement

The Wheels on the Bus

Those wheels keep going round and round.

Materials
*Words to the song
(See below.)*

Activity
Once you are familiar with the song, "The Wheels on the Bus," add some movement. Lay your baby on his back and try the movements suggested below.

The Wheels on the Bus

The wheels on the bus go round and round, round and round, round and round. *(Circle baby's legs around.)*

The wheels on the bus go round and round, all over town.

The doors on the bus go open and shut, open and shut, open and shut. *(Open baby's arms wide out from his chest and then cross them back over.)*

The doors on the bus go open and shut, all over town.

The wipers on the bus go swish, swish, swish—swish, swish, swish—swish, swish, swish. *(Move baby's legs from side to side.)*

The wipers on the bus go swish, swish, swish, all over town.

The horn on the bus goes beep, beep, beep—beep, beep, beep—beep, beep, beep. *(Tap baby's belly button.)*

The horn on the bus goes beep, beep, beep, all over town.

The mommies (daddies) on the bus say "I love you, I love you, I love you." *(Give baby lots of kisses.)*

The mommies (daddies) on the bus say "I love you," all over town.

Music and Movement

The Hokey Pokey

Materials

Words to the song
(See below.)

Activity

The Hokey Pokey is traditionally done in a large circle with many people participating. But with your baby, you will have to do it differently. With baby lying down, start to sing the first line, "You put your right arm in." Gently pick up his right arm, and cross it over his body. When the line says, "You take your right arm out," take his arm and place it down gently. When you say, "You shake it all about," gently wave baby's arm. Do the same for the left arm and the right and left legs. With the line, "You do the Hokey Pokey and you turn yourself around," roll baby's hands over each other. As baby begins to stand, try adding body parts like his head and his backside. He may surprise you at how quickly he responds.

(This can be a great "getting dressed" exercise, too. As you put the baby's arms and legs into his clothes, sing the appropriate line.)

The Hokey Pokey

You put your right (left) arm in, you put your right (left) arm out,

You put your right (left) arm in, and you shake it all about.

You do the hokey pokey and you turn yourself around,

And that's what it's all about.

Music and Movement

Ring Around the Rosy

Try this before and after baby is standing.

Materials

*Words to the song
(See below.)*

Activity

Since you often sit with your baby, it is fun to get up and move around. Moving to nursery rhymes and poems is an enjoyable way to do them. The movement to this traditional poem has everyone holding hands, moving in a circle, and falling down. But with a young baby, you should cuddle her in your arms, sing the song, and walk or dance slowly in a circle. When you get to the "We all fall down" line, plop into the nearest comfortable chair and watch your baby smile.

Ring Around the Rosy

Ring around the rosy,

A pocket full of posies.

Ashes, ashes, we all fall down.

Music and Movement

Making Circles

Materials

None

Activity

Let your baby have fun while movement is taking place. This is often a good activity while getting baby dressed or changed. With a young baby lying down, gently circle baby's arms in the air and say, "Alex is making circles with his arms." Then move his legs in circles and say, "Alex is making circles with his legs." Alternate the right leg and the left. As baby gets older, try an arm and a leg at the same time.

Pots and Pans Music

Older babies love this homemade band.

Materials

Pots, pans, and lids
Wooden spoons

Activity

Let your baby begin to "bang" out a tune early. Give her a collection of a few pots, pans, and lids. Let her clap the lids together or pound the spoon against the pots. A delightful family activity is to let everyone take a kitchen instrument and make music together.

Music and Movement

Outdoor Concerts

Materials

Stroller, baby carrier, or blanket
Outside concert

Activity

In many communities, outdoor concerts are held in the summertime. Audiences are often encouraged to take picnics. Check your local paper to find out about an inexpensive or free concert in a nearby park or amphitheater. These concerts are usually casual, with people sitting on the ground. Once you have chosen a concert, pack up your baby and go. Make sure you have enough bottles, toys, food, or any other paraphernalia you might need. Try to find a seat toward the back or the edge of the seating area. This way, if baby becomes fussy, you can move her out quickly. Our girls enjoyed watching the people, as well as the music, and quickly won the hearts of those surrounding them.

My Very Own Tape

This may become a family treasure.

Materials

Blank tape
Tape recorder
Baby's favorite songs

Activity

After listening to tapes and records, choose some that you particularly enjoy. These do not all have to be children's songs. Then, tape the favorite records. Before you tape these songs for your baby, record a brief introduction for the tape. Make sure you include her name in your introduction. Then, play the tape for her. This is great to take along in the car, but be sure to make a duplicate. Ours broke because we played it so often.

16

Music and Movement

The Noble Duke of York

This is a bouncy favorite.

Materials

Words to the song (See below.)

Activity

Learn the words to this song before beginning so you can concentrate on watching your baby's face as he moves up and down the hill. With a little baby, just cradle her in your arms. As you say the word "up," gently swing her up with your arms. When you say "down," swing her down. When you say "half way up," swing her back and forth. Older babies will enjoy this if you sit them on your knee. Hold them firmly under the arms. As you say, "marched them up the hill," raise your knee, and when you say, "marched them down again," lower your knee. For the second verse, again, raise baby up and down as the words say, but move him rapidly up and down for "neither up nor down." This was a true favorite with our girls. We found we needed a chair that supported our backs well.

The Noble Duke of York

The noble Duke of York,
He had ten thousand men.
He marched them up the hill,
And then he marched them down again.
For when you're up, you're up,
And when you're down, you're down.
But when you're only half way up,
You're neither up nor down.

17

Music and Movement

Where Is Thumbkin?

Materials

Words to the song
(See below.)

Activity

The movement to this song involves using both hands at the same time. Your baby needs to be able to see you while you sing and perform the movements for him. Start out with both hands behind your back. Begin by singing "Where is thumbkin?" As you sing, "Here I am, here I am," bring out your right hand and wiggle your thumb for the baby. When you sing, "Here I am, here I am" again, bring your left hand from behind your back and wiggle your left thumb. This is more effective if you curl your other fingers so only your thumb is showing. In the next lines, the Thumbkins talk to each other by saying, "How are you today, sir? Very well, I thank you. Run away, run away." As your fingers talk to each other, wiggle them, and then place the right hand behind your back as he runs away and then do the same with your left hand. Repeat this for each of your fingers, pointer, tall man, ring man, and pinkie. For very little babies, or for a change of pace with an older baby, sing the verse and wiggle each of their fingers as you mention its name.

Where Is Thumbkin?

Where is Thumbkin?
Where is Thumbkin?
Here I am, here I am.
How are you today, sir?
Very well, I thank you.
Run away, run away.
The next verses begin
Where is Pointer?
Where is Tall Man?
Where is Ring Man?
Where is Pinkie?'

Table of Contents for Learning Language

Learning Language
Introduction

Your baby is experiencing language even before her birth. From the moment she enters your world, language surrounds her constantly in many forms. As you speak to her, she hears your voice. Doting grandparents and siblings also contribute to the language that she hears. Taking your baby on an outing or to a gathering also exposes her to more language. If you have a television set on in the house or the radio on in the car, your baby will be further exposed to sound.

What a joy it is when our babies start making language of their own. Of course, crying is their first form of communication, but it is the initial d-d-d sounds that make parents jump for joy. When our babies really start talking and saying words we understand, we can hardly keep from shouting from the rooftops.

The seeds for talking are planted early in your baby's life, so it is important that you begin talking to your baby right from the beginning. Talk to your baby about everything. Sing to her. Read to her. Surround her with language. As she begins to make sounds, parrot them back. Her cooing should be a cue for you to coo, too.

Your voice shouldn't be the only one your baby hears. Have other people talk to her. Let her hear people with high voices, soft voices, and musical voices. She will appreciate the different voices, listening more intently to one she has never heard before.

How should you talk to your baby? Should you use baby talk? That is a decision for you to make, although we know of very few parents who can resist. However, short simple sentences will be easiest for baby to understand as she begins to comprehend what language is all about. This happens long before she utters her first sentence. As a parent, you will want to foster language development. Use the activities in this section to help you focus on this development. Whenever you're with your baby, talk to her, wherever you happen to be.

It is also important to read to your baby. Since it makes you sit with your child and focus, reading can be a calming experience in a busy day. It also helps in language development because as children hear the language, they internalize what it is supposed to sound like. Show her pictures and words. Your baby won't be reading on her own for several years, but you have the golden opportunity now to nurture a love of reading and books. Even at this age, model reading by reading yourself. If you are unsure what to read, some resource books listed on page 75 may give you some ideas.

Learning Language
Introduction *(cont.)*

Take time and read through picture books you get for your baby. Many are just as entertaining for adults as they are for babies. If you find one that is boring, then don't read it to your baby. Your boredom may well be transferred to your voice, and baby may soon tune out the words. If the book has pictures that are appealing, then show them and make up your own story. The public library is a great source for books. You can go every week with your baby and come home with a whole collection of books to share. We would check out about ten a week, and then choose three or four to share with our babies. Take your baby to the library with you. Even the littlest baby in a baby sling can enjoy the sight of all those books. Many libraries have special areas set aside for children's books and tapes. Your children's librarian may also prove a rich resource if you are having trouble deciding on a book.

Also, remember, books make wonderful gifts for babies. When asked what you might like for your baby, tell your friends and family "books!" Your collection should include a few good nursery rhyme books, a collection of children's poetry, and lots of story and picture books. Speaking and reading to your baby makes learning language a snap and so much fun to do!

Learning Language

Ba, Ba, Baby

Materials

None

Activity

Hold your baby in your arms with his face opposite yours. With a little baby, you may need to just cradle him in your arms. Begin by making soft "b" sounds, saying "ba, ba, ba." After a few times, say, "ba, ba, baby." As you say, "ba, ba, baby," bring your baby close to your face. After the word "baby," move him away and smile. Repeat until your baby loses interest.

As a variation, if mother is holding baby, say, "ma, ma, mommy," and if father is playing, say, "da, da, daddy."

Funny Sounds

Materials

None

Activity

Sit comfortably with your baby. Start by making soft sounds like blowing or soft humming. Then, make funny sounds like "cluck, cluck" or try clicking, using your tongue. As your baby grows older, you can encourage her to try to make some of the funny sounds with you.

Learning Language

What Did You Say? Say It Again.

Materials

None

Activity

Listen to your baby very closely. Is she cooing? Is she babbling? Is she repeating a sound over and over again? As she makes a sound, hold her close and repeat the sound back to her. She really is trying to talk to you, and the most appropriate response is talking back to her.

Sh, Sh, Whispering

Materials

None

Activity

If you want your baby to listen to you, sometimes you may need to get her attention. Although your baby will listen intently to you, something else may distract her. For a change of pace from your normal voice, whisper part of what you are saying. The lowering of volume will cause a different reaction from your baby. The more she hears you talk, the more language she is exposed to. Vary the speed and rhythm of your voice, as well as the volume.

Learning Language

It's All in the Name

Materials

None

Activity

Our names are special to us. Parents choose a name that they like and give it to their baby. Some babies are named after relatives or famous people. All babies like to hear their names. So, try to use your baby's name each time you speak to her. That doesn't mean you won't call her "baby" or "cutie," but if her name is Christina, then call her Christina often. If you want her to be known as Chris, then you should refer to her as Chris when she is a baby. If you take the lead in what you call your baby, others will follow suit. Before you know it, she will recognize her name and respond when you say, "Hello, Christina."

Who's That Baby?

Materials

Large mirror
A few brightly colored
  toys
Blanket

Activity

Sit with your baby or place her on a blanket near a mirror. Let her see herself, and then let her see you in the mirror. Take some of her toys and wave them so they can be seen in the mirror. Even with a very young baby who may not be looking in the mirror, point to her and say, "Who's the baby? Oh, that's Angel I see." If she doesn't seem interested in the mirror, point to the toy and say, "Oh look, a bright orange ball. Who sees that? Angel does!"

Learning Language

Read to Me

Baby is never too young to be read to.

Materials

Several books (See listing on page 77.)

Activity

Gently hold your baby or sit with your baby in your lap or next to you. Read whatever stories or poems you happen to enjoy. She will not be able to comprehend what the words mean, but she will hear the words, tones, and inflections in your voice. Read with expression in your voice, varying the pitch for various characters. Until your baby is old enough to tell you what you have missed (which won't happen in the first year), don't worry about reading every word on the page or even reading the story as it is written. As baby gets older, encourage her to look at the pictures. One activity that little ones like is when you choose a story and change one of the character's names to theirs as you read it. We feel that snuggling next to our baby while reading a favorite book is about as good as it gets. Our nine and thirteen-year-old children still enjoy reading with us.

Singing Songs

Lyrics make the heart grow fonder of the music.

Materials

Lyrics and music (See suggestions on page 76.)

Activity

Choose some favorite songs. Keep them very simple. Songs like "Row, Row, Row Your Boat" or "Dairy" are good ones. Learn the words and the music and sing them to your baby. Your baby will be able to hear language as you sing songs especially for him. A family favorite of ours was "My Favorite Things" from *The Sound of Music*.

Learning Language

Nursery Rhymes

Materials

Nursery Rhymes (See suggestions on page 77.)

Activity

Nursery rhymes are dandy to know. They can calm a cranky baby, they can make siblings laugh, and they can help baby learn language. Think back, and you will probably remember a few. Rhymes are better for little babies—the simpler the better. "Twinkle, Twinkle, Little Star" and "Humpty Dumpty" are good beginning poems for you to know. Nursery rhymes are great fun to recite in the car. Making a tape of them with your own voice is one way to keep your little one amused during short car trips. As your baby gets older, you can add other rhymes. Some babies love those that have alliteration (the repetition of the initial consonant sounds) in them. As your baby becomes older, seek out less familiar rhymes to share with him.

Twinkle, Twinkle
Twinkle, twinkle, little star,
How I wonder what you are.
Up above the world so high,
Like a diamond in the sky.
Twinkle, twinkle, little star,
How I wonder what you are.

Humpty Dumpty
Humpty Dumpty sat on a wall.
Humpty Dumpty had a great fall.
All the king's horses and all the king's men,
Couldn't put Humpty together again.

Lucy Locket
Lucy Locket lost her pocket,
Kitty Fisher found it.
Nothing in it, nothing in it,
But the binding round it.

Learning Language

This Is the Way We Put On Our Clothes

As baby gets dressed, sing this song and add some language to the morning routine.

Materials

Clothes that you dress baby in
Words to the song (See below.)

Activity

Dressing your baby can often be a difficult time. Try to distract baby with this activity. As you place arms and legs into clothing, sing this song to the tune of "Here We Go 'Round the Mulberry Bush." Your baby will be hearing the words for his body parts. As he gets older, and you ask him to put out his arm, he will understand you.

This Is the Way We Put On Our Clothes

This is the way we put on our clothes, put on our clothes, put on our clothes.
This is the way we put on our clothes, so early in the morning.
This is the way we put our head in, put our head in, put our head in.
This is the way we put our head in, so early in the morning.
This is the way we put our (left/right) arm in, put our arm in, put our arm in.
This is the way we put our arm in, so early in the morning.
This is the way we put our (left/right) leg in, put our leg in, put our leg in.
This is the way we put our leg in, so early in the morning.

Learning Language

"Read" the Menu

Brightly colored children's menus entertain baby.

Materials
Menus with pictures or placemats

Activity
While waiting for the food to come, either hold your baby in your lap or sit her in a high chair. Then, proceed to "read" the menu to your baby. Children's menus with brightly colored pictures work best. Take time to name pictures on the menu, pointing out any of the foods that you might have ordered. If you have a baby old enough to be eating anything from the menu, show her what will be coming. Read the names of the food, and then repeat it when the food comes. This will give her an opportunity to make connections with words, pictures, and objects.

Dinner Time Conversation

Don't leave baby out.

Material
Family meal
Baby carrier or high chair

Activity
In our home, dinner time has always been the time to talk and listen to each other. Before dinner, place your baby in his carrier on or near the dinner table. (Older babies can sit in high chairs.) As you have dinner time conversation, make an effort to include your baby. To even the littlest ones you can say, "Steven, how was your day?" Always use your baby's name and direct some comments to him. As he gets older and starts to make sounds, repeat those sounds back to him. Be sure to start early in the evening to make dinner time a family affair.

Learning Language

Kitty Says Meow

And the cow says moo, and the duck goes quack!

Materials

Books with pictures of animals (See suggested list on page 76.)

Activity

Choose some books that have pictures of animals. Large photographs are easier for baby to see. Sit comfortably with baby on your lap or next to you. Open the book, and find a picture of an animal that appeals to you. Repeat the sound the animal makes a few times. Do this with other animal pictures in the book.

Ring, Ring

There goes that phone again.

Materials

Telephone (both real and play)

Activity

The telephone is one of those mixed blessings. It is a fabulous communication tool. However, with a baby in the house, the phone can be an annoyance, since it seems as if everytime you are in the middle of feeding, playing, or dressing your baby, it will ring. But, the phone can fill a useful purpose in learning language.

Make a game of answering the phone. Each time it rings, say to your baby, "There's that phone, Pam. We'd better answer it." Even a little baby can sit on your lap while you speak. If you are talking to someone you think will be indulgent, before you leave the conversation give baby an opportunity to listen and "talk." Ask the person on the other end to say, "Hello, Pam. How are you today?" If baby seems interested, let the other person keep talking; otherwise, take the phone back. As your baby gets older, let her have a play phone of her own.

Learning Language

Sock Puppets

Materials

Colorful permanent markers
Clean, white socks (Large athletics socks work best.)

Activity

Take a clean, white sock. Using colorful markers, draw a simple face on it. Include eyes, eyebrows, nose, mouth, and ears. You may want to put the sock on your hand, mark everything with a pencil, and then take it off and draw the face. A nice touch is to make the eyes the same color as your baby's.

Slip the puppet on your hand. Wrap the materials so that the area covering your hand has the mouth. Show your baby the puppet. Make your puppet "talk" by moving your hand. Have your puppet "talk," telling your baby things like "I see Phillip. He has such curly hair," or "Look at Phillip, he is such a happy boy today."

Another way to play with your puppet is to point out the puppet's ears, eyes, etc., and then show your baby where his eyes and ears are located.

You can make several puppets, and let siblings participate. As baby gets older, he'll want his own puppet. Make him his own, using a small baby sock, so it fits his hand.

Learning Language

Where Is My Thumb?

The rhythm is as important as the words.

Materials

*Words to the rhyme
(See below.)*

Activity

Your baby will listen more attentively if you can make things more rhythmic. While doing this rhyme with your baby, tap out the rhythm on the edge of the table or with your foot. Emphasize the body part words as you say them. With your baby lying down or sitting with you, say the verse. As you do, find the baby's thumb and tap lightly on it. For her eyes, tap next to them. Improvise by adding more body parts as your baby seems ready to learn them.

Where Is My Thumb?

Where is my thumb?
Da, dum, da, dum.
Where is my thumb?
Da, dum, da, dum.
Where is my nose?
Ba, bum, ba, bum.
Where is my nose?
Ba, bum, ba, bum.
Where is my ear?
De, de, de, de.
Where is my ear?
De, de, de, de.
Where is my eye?
Da, die, da, die
Where is my eye?
Da, die, da, die.

Learning Language

Touch My Mouth

Materials

None

Activity
Babies are curious about mouths. Let your baby touch your mouth as your speak. Little babies will just watch your lips, but let your older baby touch your lips as you make a variety of letter sounds. Let him touch your lips as you say, "pa, ba," so he can see your lips move. Make some sounds like the "k" or "j" so he can feel air come out of your mouth. Give him the chance to see if he can figure out the vibration that "z" makes.

In the Market

Take baby and make this a language experience.

Materials

Shopping cart that can safely hold your baby

Activity
No doubt you will constantly have to take baby to the grocery store with you. Make this outing rich with language. Secure your baby in a carrier or a seat in the basket. (Many markets today provide special carriers for babies too young to sit up.) With your baby in your basket and your shopping list in hand, amble through the market, making lots of stops along the way.

When you get to the produce department, point to or pick up a red apple, and say to your baby, "Look Cathy, this is a red shiny apple. See how round it is." At the dairy department show your baby some cheese and say, "This is yellow cheese. It's cut into a square shape." Have fun on the aisle that has baby food by showing your baby all the pictures of the babies on the products. When you come to the pet aisle, ask your baby what the dog says as you show her a can of dog food that has a picture of a pooch on it. As your baby gets older you can let her hold onto something that you intend to buy.

Table of Contents for Playing Games

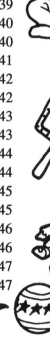

Playing Games
Introduction

Peek-a-boo, I see you! What parents haven't instinctively played this game with their baby? Games and babies seem made for each other, since almost anything you do with a baby can become a game.

The games in this section are intended to stretch your game playing with baby when you know that you want to play a game but just can't think of one more. The few materials needed are simple, easy to find around the house, and may even recycle some existing items. While you are playing with your baby, remember that he is not going to know the rules. As a matter of fact, games with babies have only one rule, and that is to have fun. As you interact with your baby, keep in mind that he may not enjoy what you are doing at the moment. If he fusses, don't attempt to go on; you can always try again later. Sometimes a few seconds is as long as a baby can really play. That's perfectly okay. The younger your baby is, the less he will play. Don't expect the same response from a three-month-old that you will get from a nine-month-old. With a younger baby, it is perfectly acceptable to do all the "work" while he just watches and listens.

On the other hand, sometimes a game is just what a cranky baby needs to cheer him up. If he seems fretful because he is bored, then some interaction may do the trick. Some of the games require more action than others. Some will be more fun with baby in your arms, while others will work well if baby can sit up or move around. Only you will know your baby well enough to know if you need an active game or a quiet one.

Most of all, relax and enjoy playing games with your baby. Our experience tells us that there is not a more enjoyable playmate in the world than your very own baby.

Playing Games

Diaper Wiper Box

Recycle that box, and let baby have lots of fun with it.

Materials

Cleaned diaper wiper box with hinged lid
Blocks
Rattles

Activity

Put various items into a cleaned diaper wiper box that has an attached hinged lid. With a young baby, you may put the items in yourself, showing each one to baby and telling her what it is. Show an older baby how to open the lid, and have her drop in as many items as she can. Give her the opportunity to open the lid, take out everything, and then put everything back in.

Peek-a-Boo, I See You

This classic game is still great fun for you and baby!

Materials

Handkerchief

Activity

With baby sitting or lying down, place a handkerchief in front of your face. For very young babies, it is especially important not to cover baby's face. As you remove the handkerchief from your face, gently say, "peek-a-boo." As your baby gets older, this game can be played in various ways, including letting the baby cover your face.

Playing Games

Texture Box

Materials

Box

Large scraps of
  various textured
  materials (velvet,
  felt, silk, flannel)

Activity

Prepare a texture box by placing scraps of various textured fabrics into a box. With a younger baby, take the fabric out and let her touch each piece. You can gently touch her arm with it. With an older baby, let her take the fabric out of the box herself. Have her touch the fabric at the same time you touch it. Describe the material to her as soft, rough, smooth, or whatever is appropriate but simple.

Rattle Play

Don't just shake those rattles; help baby find them by listening.

Materials

Rattles that make
  different sounds

Activity

When your baby is lying or sitting down, pick up a rattle so he cannot see it. Shake it next to his ear, and when he turns tell him that he has found the rattle. Try this with different rattles. As baby gets older, use more than one rattle, and see if he can find them. Let him try shaking the rattle next to your ear, and tell him when you hear the rattle.

Playing Games

Balls in the Bowl

Materials

Large, clear plastic bowl

Two to three plastic balls or colored tennis balls

Activity

Place two or three tennis balls into a large, clear plastic bowl. Place baby next to the bowl where she can see. Gently swirl the balls in the bowl, telling baby to look at the balls. With an older baby, give her the balls to drop into the bowl. Show her how to move the bowl, and with your help, let her try.

Pull Toys

Materials

Pull toy that makes noise

Activity

Chances are you received a pull toy as a baby present. Your baby is too young to play with it as intended. However, he is not too young for you to play with him. With baby lying or sitting, pull the toy in front of him so he can see it. Pull it in one direction and then the other. Make it go fast and slow, and tell him, "Now, I'm pulling this fast. Now, I'm pulling this slowly."

A pull toy that makes noise will make this more exciting for baby. As he gets older, let him pull the string to bring the toy to him. He may want to try pulling the string as he begins walking.

Playing Games

Smile

This is a game ready-made for siblings to play with baby.

Materials
None

Activity
From the first time you look at your baby, you will smile. You will need to wait about six to eight weeks to have baby smile back.

As your baby grows, make it a game to smile at her in all different ways. Sometimes smile widely; other times show your teeth. Put your face close to hers and other times back away. Carefully watch baby's response and see which smile she likes best.

Tin Foil Ball

It is light weight, handy, and easy to dispose of.

Materials
Tin foil

Activity
Take a large amount of tin foil and crumple it into a ball. Make sure it is a ball much too large to fit into baby's mouth. Roll the ball to a little baby, or toss it up in the air for baby to see. Let older babies drop this ball from high chairs since it will cause no damage. Monitor the ball. It is not a toy for baby to play with unsupervised. If it starts to tear, throw it out.

Playing Games

Toe Wiggle

Materials

None

Activity

This activity works well just before putting socks or shoes on your baby or right after a bath. Even with the littlest baby, look down at her bare feet and say, "Where are your toes?" As you say, "Here are your toes," gently wiggle her toes. As baby gets older she will start to reach for her own toes.

For a variation of this game you will need to sit barefoot with your baby. Gently wiggle your own toes as you say, "Where are my toes? Here they are." As your baby gets older, let her find and wiggle your toes for you.

More Toe Fun

This traditional game will surely amuse baby.

Materials

*Words to the poem
(See below.)*

Activity

You can wiggle your baby's toes as you recite this classic poem. It is best done with a barefoot baby, but we've tried it with socks on, and it works just as well.

This Little Piggy

This little piggy went to market.
This little piggy stayed home.
This little piggy had roast beef.
This little piggy had none.
And this little piggy cried wee, wee, wee,
All the way home.

Playing Games

Hat Try On

Get the camera ready for this one.

Materials

Box or basket for storage
Different types of hats (large sun hat, baseball cap, bonnet, beret)
Mirror

Activity

Fill a box or basket with several hats so they're handy. With your baby looking at you, reach into the box and try a hat on your head. Then, ask baby if she wants to try one on. Gently place the hat from your head onto hers. Be careful; it will probably slip over her eyes and she may not like this. Then, put another hat on your head and together look in the mirror, pointing out your hat.

If she will let you, put different hats on her, looking at each in the mirror. If she likes this game enough, she may even agree to wear a hat outside for more than 30 seconds at a time!

Toes and Nose

Play this game to find baby's toes and nose.

Materials

Words to the rhyme (See below.)

Activity

Finding toes and noses is endlessly fascinating for babies. Make it fun as you use this rhyme to help baby find his nose and then his toes. Before you say any line, clap twice. Then, as you say, "Here is my nose," touch baby's nose with both your hand and baby's. Do the same with toes if baby is in a position that allows him to touch his toes comfortably.

(Clap, Clap) Where is my nose?
(Clap, Clap) Here is my nose.
(Clap, Clap) Where are my toes?
(Clap, Clap) Here are my toes.

Playing Games

Pat-a-Cake

This is a classic with a twist.

Materials

Nursery rhyme (See below.)

Activity

Chances are you will remember the classic nursery rhyme "Pat-a-Cake." But, in case you need a refresher course, it goes like this:

> Pat-a-cake, pat-a-cake,
> Baker's man.
> Bake me a cake,
> As fast as you can.
> Roll it, and pat it,
> And mark it with a B.
> Put it in the oven,
> For baby and me.

By itself, this is an enjoyable rhyme to teach your baby, but try this version along with the hand movements indicated. This became our children's favorite as they smiled and began to recognize their names. It goes like this:

Pat-a-cake, pat-a-cake *(gently clap your hands or gently hold baby's hands and clap them)*
Baker's man.
Bake me a cake,
As fast as you can.
Roll it, and pat it, *(Rotate hands over each other.)*
And mark it with a J *(Add first letter of baby's name and draw it on her tummy.)*
Put it in the oven,
For Joanna and me. *(Substitute baby's name.)*

Playing Games

Cuddle Bug

Cuddling is so much fun!

Materials

None

Activity

This is an anytime activity, but we liked it best when the girls were ready for bed. Pick your baby up, and say to her, "Let's play cuddle bug." When she is very little, just hold her in your arms and cuddle her. When she is older, let her sit next to you and cuddle.

Crowded Subway

Who's going in what direction?

Materials

None

Activity

This is best done with two people. Place a baby who can sit up in between you and the other person. One of you say, "This is a crowded subway. I'm going this way," while the other person says, "I'm going this way." As you say this, very gently scoot in close to baby. Our children's grandparents loved to play this game with our kids.

Playing Games

Up, Up in the Air

Materials

Brightly colored balls
Blanket

Activity

Gently lay your baby down on the blanket. Then, toss a brightly colored ball up in the air so your baby can see you catch it. As baby begins to sit up, you may throw more than one ball. Let him play with it if he reaches for it.

Climb over the Mountain

Crawling babies think this is a great adventure.

Materials

Pillows of various sizes and shapes

Activity

This is fun once your baby is crawling. Place many pillows on the floor. Let your baby crawl over the pillows. For a variation, move the pillows around and encourage baby to crawl in a different direction.

Playing Games

Pass It

Materials
Small toy

Activity
Sit opposite your baby with a small toy in your hand. Make sure it is a toy that can be gripped easily. Pass it over to your baby and keeping your hand on the toy say, "Zach, please pass the toy back." Your baby will have no idea what you are requesting, but as you say, "Pass the toy back," take the toy and say, "What a good job! Shall we try again?" If your baby approximates giving you the toy, praise him. He may also want to keep the toy after the first pass, and that's fine. It will take your baby awhile to learn this game, but it is the very beginning of sharing.

What's in My Pocket?

Always keep a mirror handy.

Materials
Unbreakable pocket mirror
Comb
Credit cards

Activity
When our children were little, we found a pocket mirror and a comb indispensable to have with us to create new games as we needed them.

Occasionally, you may have to wait someplace with your baby and need to amuse her. If you make sure to always carry a few items, you can just dig into your pocket and pull something out. A little baby may like the feel of a soft-bristled brush on his hair, while an older baby may be fascinated by looking at herself in the mirror. Credit cards can be used to shuffle and toss. Change some of the items, or get them in a few different colors, so baby can feel a sense of surprise each time you play.

Playing Games

Bat the Toys

A toy tied to the wall makes changing your baby so much easier.

Materials

Bright ribbon
Nails or hooks
Toys that can be tied
  (rattles with handles
  and soft dolls)

Activity

Begin by tying a brightly colored ribbon securely onto each toy, preferably through the handle. Then, with a nail or hook, attach the toy to the wall next to the changing table. Before you change baby, set the toys in motion. As your baby gets older, encourage him to touch the toys. He may try to bat them around with his feet or hands. Frequently change the toys which are tied to the ribbon. For safety's sake, keep the ribbons short, not more than three or four inches. Nail them low enough for baby to reach the toy and swing it.

It amazed us how quickly our daughters managed to start batting the toys around. They especially liked rattles in primary colors.

Pick It Up

Fun for baby, great exercise for grown ups.

Materials

High chair
Objects that can be
  dropped (balls,
  clothespins, blocks)

Activity

At around six months, your baby will delight in not only dropping items while sitting in a high chair, but also in having them returned to him. Although this is a game that your little one will think is okay to play at mealtimes, give him very specific objects to drop and tell him, "These are what we drop, not the spoon."

Playing Games

Moving Place Mats

With baby sitting on a lap or in a high chair, this is an activity full of fun.

Materials

Lightweight, colorful placemats (Cloth ones are best.)

Activity

This is a good activity to use just before setting the table. Put two or more placemats out on an empty table. Sit down with your baby in your lap. Pull one of the placemats toward you. Now, give your baby a chance to pull the placemat. Switch the positions of the placemats by shuffling them around. Do not pick them up. Watch to see if your baby notices the changing of the positions. Help him move the placemats until he can do it himself. Don't be surprised if he just picks up a placemat and starts to play peek-a-boo. Our children found placemats just the right size and weight to do this as they got older.

Coaster Shuffle

Materials

A set of four to six coasters (They don't have to match.)

Activity

Sit with your baby near a low table. If your baby is older, this is a good activity to do standing up. Let your baby begin playing with coasters by just showing them to him. Our children's favorites were round plastic ones with bright colors and birds on them. Stack the coasters and then take each individually and stack it on the table. Then, restack the coasters. Let older babies try to restack the coasters by themselves. If there is a coaster holder, let baby try putting them into it.

Playing Games

Knock 'em Down

While eating out, this can make a difference in how long you can stay at the table.

Materials
Individual jelly containers, sugar packs, or creamers

Activity
While very young babies may sleep in their carriers while you go out to eat, older ones will need to be entertained. This is a good game to play, especially at a coffee shop that has individual packets of jam, jelly, or creamers on the table. With your baby on your lap or in a high chair, take a few of the jelly containers and stack them up. Then, knock them down. Next, try building your tower higher so that your baby can help you knock it down. Even some young babies will be excited if you help them gently topple the tower. If you prefer not to let your baby knock the tower down, then just do the first part and take it down yourself. We always made sure the packets were well sealed and then left a large tip!

Copy Cat

Do as I do.

Materials
None

Activity
Take advantage of your little one's desire to imitate you. Show her what you are doing, such as rubbing your tummy or touching your hands on the table. Tell her, "I'm rubbing my hands together, now. Can you do the same?" Then do it, and encourage her to try.

Try many different movements including touching your nose, patting your hair, or stroking your cheek.

Table of Contents for The Great Outdoors

The Great Outdoors
Introduction

Babies, blankets, and balls all seem made for the great outdoors. While we, as adults, may define the great outdoors as the mountains, the seashore, or the desert, for a little child, the great outdoors may be as simple as a plot of grass in the yard.

Your baby will enjoy the change of scenery that being outdoors brings. Take advantage of parks, outside malls, nature trails, and, of course, your own backyard. Make being outdoors as comfortable as possible. Dress your baby in appropriate clothing. If it is a cold day, make sure your baby is warm enough, adding hats and mittens if necessary. On sunny days, be sure to add a sun hat and sunblock that is made for baby's sensitive skin.

Keep a blanket or a beach towel handy, stored with your baby supplies. This way, if a tree swaying in the wind or a lush lawn should summon you unexpectedly, you'll be prepared. While some of the activities found in this section can be done indoors, take advantage of doing them outside, using natural resources, such as leaves or sea shells. You'll want to leave any area the way you found it, so if an activity calls for a leaf, find one on the ground rather than picking it from a tree.

For less mobile babies, lying or sitting on a blanket will be easy. But, as your baby begins to crawl and walk, remember to take great care outside. Sand at the beach will provide a less smooth surface to walk on; rocks can easily be picked up and thrown or swallowed. Little hands will want to investigate the great outdoors. Allow your little one as much freedom as possible to explore, but keep an eye out to avoid hazards.

Many activities found in other sections of this book can be transferred to the outdoors. Many of the games that you play with baby can be played under a tree, or you may just wish to read a book outside. Use your discretion and common sense before transferring an indoor activity to an outdoor one.

Above all else, learn to appreciate the outdoors through the eyes of your baby. Is the sun too hot to play outside? Then, it's time to move inside. Does the wind blowing gently on baby bring a huge smile and a bigger sense of wonder? Then, grab a pinwheel or blow some bubbles and take advantage of what nature has to offer. Besides formal activities, simply enjoy the change of scenery. Point out the blue in the sky and the green in the trees. Talk about the shapes of the clouds. The great outdoors is wonderful for playing with your baby and having fun.

The Great Outdoors

Wagon Pull

Keep those wagon wheels rolling.

Materials

Wagon
Blanket or towel
Rattles or soft toys

Activity

Take your baby on an outing, using an alternative to a stroller. Use a wagon—the type with high sides is preferable. Put a blanket or towel in for comfort. If you are taking a younger baby for a walk, lay her down. As the baby lies on her back, show her the trees or houses that you pass. With an older baby, let her sit up and look around. As you pull the wagon, point out things nearby, giving baby a chance to touch those that she can easily reach. If your baby gets restless, let her play with the toys you have brought along so you can extend your trip.

Leaf Tickle

Watch baby's face light up as you gently tickle him.

Materials

Variety of large leaves
Blanket or towel

Activity

With your baby sitting or lying on a large blanket, show him leaves from various trees. After checking that the leaves do not have sharp edges, gently stroke your baby's arms, legs, or tummy. An older baby may "tickle" you with the leaf. As you touch your baby, talk to him, and tell him that you are going to touch his arm or tickle his tummy. Repeat this with several different types of leaves, giving your baby a different sensation with each one.

The Great Outdoors

Touch a Tree

Watch your baby delight in the wonder of trees.

Materials

Trees with low lying branches

Activity

Take your baby in your arms, and show her a tree. Tell her about the colors of the leaves and the trunk. Gently let her touch the trunk of the tree. Talk about the different textures, describing the leaves as soft and the trunk as rough. Holding your baby securely, shake a low lying branch, and let her grab (although not remove) the leaves on the lowest branches. Give an older baby the opportunity to shake the branch. If you can hear birds in the tree, bring the sounds to her attention by asking her if she can hear the birds.

What's That Creepy Crawly?

Creepy crawlies are fascinating creatures.

Materials

Blanket
Creepy crawlies such as ants, snails, and crickets

Activity

Find a place in a yard or on the sidewalk where some type of creepy crawling critters live. Holding your baby at a safe distance (one where she can see, but not touch), let her look at the parade of ants or a cricket jumping. Perhaps, you will be fortunate and see a worm crawling in the earth or a snail lumbering across a sidewalk. Show these animals to your baby, explaining to her that they are part of nature. If your child is walking, hold her hand and let her follow the creepy crawlies, making as many stops along the way as she finds necessary to investigate these creatures.

The Great Outdoors

Bubbles, Bubbles

Watch the bubbles go pop.

Materials

*Non-toxic bubble
  solution and wand
Blanket*

Activity
Place your baby on a blanket on a grassy area. Show your baby the jar of bubble solution and the bubble wand. Gently blow bubbles so baby can see them. (Do not blow them directly toward baby's face.) As they drift by, point them out to younger babies, saying, "See the bubbles? They are round. Soon they'll pop and disappear." As baby gets older, he may want to try to blow or catch bubbles. Help him to do this, but do not allow him to handle bubble solution as it may sting his eyes.

In the Sky

Look up; look down; look up again.

Materials

Blanket

Activity
Together, side by side, lie on your back on a blanket. Now, look up in the sky, making sure that the sun is below the horizon or behind an obstruction. Talk to your baby as you begin to point out all the things there are to see—clouds, buildings, birds, and wires, even a helicopter or plane if you are lucky. If you see a plane, make a sound like one. As you see each new sight, describe it for your baby in short simple sentences. "Look at the big, white cloud." "A silver airplane just went by." "That blue house is where we live." Younger babies may just listen and look, while older babies may want to point with you. Encourage them and describe whatever they might point out.

The Great Outdoors

Roll Over and Over

Round and round and round it goes.

Materials

*Balls of different sizes
Blanket or beach
    towel*

Activity

Spread your blanket on the grass. Place your baby on
the blanket in a sitting position. Sit a short distance
apart, facing him. Gently roll the ball to your baby. Let
your baby pick up the ball and explore it. If your baby
is older, he may be able to push it back to you. To vary
the activity, use different-sized balls and sit further
away. A ball with bells in it will bring a special delight
to the activity as your baby tries to figure out where the
noise is coming from.

Tummy Delight

Outside on the lawn, this is great fun!

Materials

*Large, sturdy ball
Blanket*

Activity

Place the ball on the blanket. Hold your baby securely
and, not letting go, place her tummy on the ball. Gently
let her roll back and forth, lifting her or sliding her
carefully off the ball. Repeat a few times. For a
change, use an inflated, tubular-shaped cylinder that
rolls.

The Great Outdoors

Playing with a Pinwheel

Bright and shiny, a breeze makes these amazing to watch.

Materials
Pinwheel
Blanket

Activity
Seat or lay your baby on a blanket outside. Take out the pinwheel so your baby can see it. Then, move it back, so the wind can catch it. If it is not a windy day, you will have to blow it or move it back and forth to keep it spinning. Tell your baby, "This is a pinwheel. See how Daddy can make it go?" With a younger baby, you might wish to place the pinwheel in the ground where the baby can watch it spinning. You can let your older baby "help" you blow or move your hand to make it spin. The baby should not do this alone, however, because the pinwheel might hurt her.

Cups, Cups, Cups

Materials
Several paper or plastic cups
Sand or water
Blanket

Activity
Take several unbreakable cups into the yard. Fill them with sand or water. Place baby on a blanket. With younger babies, simply pour sand or water from a full cup to an empty one. Change the height from which you pour to change the look of the stream. You might want to pour some on her hand, but be careful in doing this, so she doesn't get any in her eyes or nose. With an older baby who is sitting up, begin the same way by letting her watch you pour from one cup to another. Then, let her try. Start by holding her hand and showing her how to pour and then letting her try alone.

The Great Outdoors

Take a Hike!

Let baby join a family adventure.

Materials

*Backpack, baby
  pouch, or sling
Hat for baby*

Activity

Your family hikes or walks don't have to stop because
you have a baby. Simply take her along. When she's
very little, put her in a sling or pouch. As baby gets
older and can sit, transfer her to a baby backpack.
Practice loading her into the backpack. It is also
extremely important to follow directions for securing
her. Take care, if you are hiking on a trail, to maintain
your own footing. Also, make sure that trees, or
anything that might hit her or that she might pull, are
out of the way.

Family Social Outings

Don't give up outings because of your little one.

Materials

*Blanket
Toys
Anything appropriate
  for picnic*

Activity

Yes, it is a chore, getting all the baby's paraphernalia
into the car, but he will probably enjoy being with many
people. If you want your baby to feel comfortable
around groups of people, it is never too early to start.
Put his blanket on the outside of the group, so no one
will step on or fall over him. Monitor the number of
people who surround him at any one time. But, if he is
having a good time, don't keep people away. Have
friends pick up toys and show them to the baby. This
will encourage baby to realize that other people besides
his parents can make him feel comfortable and happy.

The Great Outdoors

The Playground

Materials
A playground with swings, slides and other equipment

Activity
Playgrounds are not designed for babies. They are usually constructed with older toddlers in mind. But, chances are you will take your baby to the playground long before he can safely swing or use the teeter-totter. Make this an enjoyable time by taking advantage of being outdoors. Hold your baby as you survey the playground. Let him watch the children swinging. You may want to hold him and swing with him. Hold him firmly, so he doesn't wiggle away. Baby bucket swings are good if your baby is actually sitting up without your support. We always put our girls into them with their legs going through the straps. Keep your hands and eyes on baby at all times.

If you enjoy sliding and can safely climb up the ladder with baby, then hold him in your lap and slide down. A playground provides outdoor fun as long as you provide the supervision.

Squeeze Play

Because water is involved, this is good outdoor activity for a warm day.

Materials
Sponges soaked in water

Activity
Sit with your baby on the lawn. Have several water-soaked sponges. With a little baby, gently squeeze some water onto his arms and legs. See what his reaction is. If yours is a baby who doesn't like this, stop here. If, however, your baby enjoys this, continue playing. With an older baby, show him how to squeeze the sponge, and let him have fun making puddles on the grass.

56

The Great Outdoors

Flower Power

A flower, preferrably on a bush

Activity

Let your baby experience the joy of flowers. Find a bush filled with brightly colored blooms. Make sure they are not poisonous or that they have no stickers or thorns that might hurt baby. Then, give your child an opportunity to first look, then smell and touch the flower. With a little baby, just seeing the flower bush might be enough of an activity. With an older one, let him sniff the flowers and touch the petals. If possible, pick one flower from the bush, and let baby take the flower apart petal by petal.

Enjoy the Weather

Material

Clothing appropriate for the weather
Days with different weather

Activity

You will, more than likely, have to take your baby someplace in the rain, snow, fog, or heat, and for you, this will probably be more of a chore than a pleasure. However, your baby can experience various types of weather throughout the year as a fun-filled activity. The most important thing is to dress your baby appropriately for the weather.

The best way to do this activity is to hold your baby or put her in a stroller. This way you can talk and describe the weather. Go out in a light rain, making sure baby is in waterproof clothing. Snow is also fun; watching baby's face as she touches a light snowfall is a delight. In the sun, have her covered with sunblock and a hat. In the wind, let her move her face in various directions and feel the difference.

The Great Outdoors

The Night Sky

Watch the stars shine and moon glow.

Materials

A starry night
Blanket

Activity

Introduce your baby to the world of the night sky by taking him outside on a star-filled night. Spread a blanket on the lawn and lie back and look up at the stars. Point out the stars overhead. Even if your baby does not seem to notice the stars, being outside in the night with you is another way to experience the great outdoors.

A Beach Stroll

You are lucky if you live near a lake or seashore.

Materials

Stroller, baby
backpack, or sling

Activity

When our children were babies, we lived near the ocean. The roar of the waves and the birds flying overhead made early morning strolls a real pleasure.

We often get so caught up in getting the day started that we forget that this is an unusually peaceful time of day, especially at the beach. If you are fortunate to live near a large body of water, take advantage of the early morning hours. Place your baby into his stroller or pack and walk near the ocean. If you have your baby in a pack or sling, you can walk next to the water. Point out to baby the birds that might be on shore or overhead. Stop and listen to the water. Enjoy the serenity of the outdoors.

Table of Contents for In the House

In the House
Introduction

Your home is a veritable playground for your baby. In it are contained all the elements that baby needs for play. Not only are mom and dad built-in playmates, there are rooms to explore, closets to get into, and cribs to motor in. Your home is the most familiar place for baby. He knows early on that his needs for food, clothing, and shelter will be met here. It is also a place just crammed with things to play with.

Before you decide which activities to use in this section, take a look at your house. Is it baby friendly? Once your baby starts moving, will your house be safe? (See page 2 for safety tips.)

These activities may take a little time to set up. But, once you have done the work, the payoff is immeasurable. Your baby will coo with delight as you show him a special light or let him climb through a tunnel. Make him the main attraction at a family meal, and he'll love the kitchen long before he can crawl.

In the House

Where's the Baby?

Let those appliance boxes become tunnels for an intrepid baby explorer.

Materials

Large appliance boxes (big enough for an adult to crawl through)
Scissors or knife
Toy or rattle

Activity

Cut the ends off the appliance boxes and create a tunnel for your baby to crawl through and explore. Depending on your baby's nature, you may wish to place several boxes together to create a longer tunnel. Show your baby how to crawl through the tunnel and try it together a few times. Then, let her crawl on her own if she is willing.

For a stimulating alternative, try the following ideas.

◆ Place a toy or rattle at the end for her to find.

◆ Crawl side by side, pretending to be an animal.

◆ Go around the outside of the tunnel and wait for your baby to get to the end.

◆ Let your baby crawl through while you follow her.

In the House

"Riding" the Basket Fun

While older siblings ride a bike, baby gets to "ride" a laundry basket.

Materials

Laundry baskets
Towels or sheets
Toys

Activity
Fold up towels or sheets. Place a few at the bottom of the basket, creating a basket liner. Steadying the basket firmly so it doesn't tip (you may use your feet), place your baby in the basket. Now, take him for a ride by pulling or pushing the basket. Make sure that your baby sits or lies in the basket while it is in motion. When baby is through riding in the basket, give him a few toys, and let him continue to play in the basket.

Where Are My Socks?

Dryers are not the only ones to misplace socks.

Materials

Laundry baskets
Socks

Activity
While you are folding laundry, give your baby several different socks. Show him how to drop them into a laundry basket. Then, encourage him to drop them one at a time. For some variety, fold a few pairs of socks together and let him drop the balls of socks into the laundry basket.

In the House

Light My Room

A flashlight makes this activity fun.

Activity

Hold your baby close to you. Dim the lights in the room and then switch on the flashlight. Slowly move the light around the room, pointing it out to baby. Take some time to let her play with the flashlight, showing her what the light can do. A younger baby may not notice much, but as your baby gets older, she'll probably enjoy this so much she'll need to try it herself.

Materials
Flashlight

This Is an Elephant

Activity

Place a colorful wall hanging in your baby's room. We hung ours near the baby's crib. Make sure the hanging is placed far enough away from the crib so that if it falls off the wall, it will not fall inside the crib. Now, lift your baby and show her the quilt. Each time you do it, ask her, "Do you see this animal? This is an elephant." Choose different animals and talk about them.
Eventually, baby will be able to help you point out the animals.

Materials
Large colorful wall hanging or picture with animals
Hammer and nails to hang it

In the House

What's on the Ceiling?

Materials

Stick-on decals
Decorations cut from
  wallpaper
Wallpaper glue
Brightly colored paint

Activity

When decorating your baby's room, don't forget the ceiling! (A baby spends so much time lying on his back that this activity will help keep him amused.) Use commercial decals, brightly colored paints, or cutouts from leftover wallpaper. Affix them to the ceiling in baby's room. Make sure they are visible from the crib when he is on his back. When you put baby to bed, point out the stars or clowns overhead. Our children had teddy bears and clouds. In the morning or after his nap, your baby will have something to look at until you can get to him.

Through the Tube

Watch baby wonder where the cloth went.

Materials

Paper towel,
  bathroom tissue, or
  mailing tube
Cloth napkin

Activity

This is an activity that is great in the kitchen when you have to amuse baby for a very short time. It uses easily accessible kitchen materials and takes about two seconds to organize. Stuff a cloth napkin into a paper towel tube. Show baby the tube but not the towel. Then, slowly pull the cloth out. An older baby will want to see the towel. Show him how to stuff the cloth and pull it out. Let him see the edge of the cloth as he watches you pull it out.

In the House

Mix It Up!

Once baby can grasp a spoon, she can help you "cook."

Materials

*A cold dish such as
cake batter that
needs stirring
Wooden spoon with a
long handle*

Activity

Hold your baby firmly or let baby sit in your lap. Show
her how you stir something. Let her hold the spoon
with you and stir together. She may lose interest after
the first stir, so don't do this activity if you really need
to get that cake made right away. Singing this little
song to "Here We Go 'Round the Mulberry Bush"
makes the activity more fun.

This is the way we mix our cake, mix our cake, mix our
cake.
This is the way we mix our cake,
All on a Saturday morning.

Making Guacamole

Pound, stir, mix, and have fun!

Activity

As your baby gets a little older, let him make guacamole
or any other dish which requires a lot of physical
activity to make. Set him up in a high chair, on the
floor, or in your lap. Show him how to pound, stir, and
mix with the spoon. Since the spoon will be out of the
bowl as often as in it, keep in mind that this can get
pretty noisy. Experience has taught us that it is worth
finding a wooden bowl and spoon to let your baby play
with. Not only will they not break as easily as some
others, but they are also a lot less noisy.

Materials

*Wooden bowl
Wooden spoon*

65

In the House

Baby Cabinet

Give baby a spot to call his own.

Materials

*Empty drawer or
    cabinet*

Activity

This is an activity for an older baby—one who can sit and crawl. The most obvious room in the house in which to have a baby cabinet is the kitchen. You can stock this with old pot lids and pans, some plastic spoons, and measuring cups and spoons. Baby will love how they nest inside one another. You are not limited to the kitchen, however, and may decide that the living room or your bedroom is better. If you are fortunate enough to have lots of rooms and drawers, then let your baby have more than one. Stock them with items that aren't found with baby's regular toys. An old hat, a pair of socks, and a few old catalogs can make these really special for baby.

Book Baskets

Every room in the house should have one.

Materials

*Books for baby (See
    suggestions on page
    76.)
Catalogs
Magazines
Baskets*

Activity

For each room in your house, create a special book basket. Fill it with picture books, magazines, and old catalogs. If you want an activity to do quickly, grab a book and your baby, and sit down and read. Your baby won't be much interested in anything more than the pictures, so it might be a good time to catch up on those magazines and catalogs which have been collecting dust. As baby gets older, make sure you have picture books and some beginning story books.

In the House

Touring Home

Home to a small baby can be the best trip.

Materials
Your home

Activity
Anywhere in your home becomes a tourist attraction for baby if you take the time to point things out. When your baby is very little, wrap him up in your arms and take him on a tour. Go into different rooms and point out the lights on the ceiling, Grandma's picture, and the cuckoo clock. Just getting the feel of the house can help a new baby become acclimated to his surroundings. As your baby grows older, take another trip, showing him things that might be of interest, pictures of the family, the dog's dish, or where the computer is located. Your baby will quickly know his home and grow to love it.

Table of Contents for Special Occasions

Special Occasions
Introduction

Having a baby in your life is new and special. Her first year is a time filled with many memorable moments. There will be special occasions that you will want to remember. There will also be times when you want your baby to be part of a major celebration. This might be a holiday, a family picnic, or a sibling's birthday party. Whatever the occasion, there are ways to make this a more memorable time for everyone concerned.

What will your baby wear to this gathering? Comfort above all else should be your guideline. If you opt for frilly, fussy clothes that baby has never worn before, expect that your baby may not be happy when she is unable to move around as much as she normally can. If a headband or a hat goes on a baby who doesn't normally wear one and you put it on just before walking in the door, expect it to last about 30 seconds.

If this is an occasion to honor someone special, such as for a graduation or birthday, then a special gift from your baby may be in order. Even a young baby can put her hand into some paint and create something as a gift.

At a large gathering of people, set the guidelines early as to how your baby will be made a part of it. Will you let others hold your baby, or will you be uncomfortable letting this happen? Determine your feelings about this and set the ground rules before the party begins. You can soothe those people who are insistent by telling them that you are just too new at this to let the baby go to other people. If it's not your first child, then just tell them you are relearning what it is like to be a parent and just cannot let this baby out of your arms. We often felt like this!

Chances are there may be cameras, both video and still. You can be patient with the photographers and still keep your baby's best interest at heart. Does everyone really need another picture of the baby with a bow in her hair? If she is fussy, you have an obligation to your baby to tell others that her modeling work is over for the day.

Take extra note of the safety of the house if it is not your own. If your baby is crawling or walking, what can she get into? Are there electrical outlets that you need to be concerned about? Is the bathroom closet easy for a baby to open? Is there a tablecloth ready to be pulled? With all this to be concerned about, how can you enjoy this special time? The trick here is to scout out the situation. It may be as simple as asking a host or hostess to close a door.

Special Occasions

Choosing Presents

When baby chooses the gift, it makes it special.

Materials

Pair of socks
Stroller
Store that sells socks

Activity

Make sure your baby is securely strapped into his stroller and take him shopping. Let your baby choose a pair of socks as a gift for someone special in his life. In many department stores, the socks are low enough for an older baby to reach while sitting in a stroller. You will need to hold a younger baby. You may need to check the sock size to make sure it is correct, but do make sure the recipient gets the same ones that baby selected. (Even if the socks are not what the recipient might wear, we can bet that he will keep them when you tell him who selected the gift.) This is how both of our children chose a gift for their first Father's Day.

On This Day You Did...

Through the years, you will treasure the notes you jot down to remember how baby celebrated a variety of firsts.

Materials

Large sticky notes
Pens or pencils
Journal

Activity

Babies do adorable things. They smile, they reach for your earrings, and they put funny hats on their heads. Often you want to remember when they did these things. Keep several sticky pads around the house along with pens or pencils. When your baby does something you want to remember, make a note of it. Date the note and place it in a journal. Some day when you have time, you can actually record all the firsts in the journal.

Special Occasions

Wrapping Presents

Special gift wrap makes the paper as much a gift as its contents.

Materials

Newsprint
Tempera paint
A few drops of liquid detergent
Small bowl or margarine tub
Butcher paper or oil cloth
Baby wipes or washcloths and soap
Tape
Scissors

Activity

This activity is messy but worth the effort. Put a few sheets of newspaper or oil cloth on the ground or on a table. Pour paint into a small bowl and add a few drops of liquid dishwashing detergent. Place it and the newsprint onto the cloth. Gently place your baby's hand into the paint. Tell your baby the color of the paint. Talk about how it feels—wet and cool. Now, lightly place your baby's hand on the newsprint in several different spots. Take great care to not let the baby get paint near his mouth or eyes. When the paper has been decorated—three or four handprints are plenty—wash baby's hands. (This can be also be done using baby's bare feet.)

Place the wrapping paper some place safe to dry before wrapping a gift with it. Be sure to write on the paper baby's name and the date the paper was created. It may be the only time when the wrapping is a bigger hit than the gift. We have even seen our baby's wrapping paper framed and mounted on the wall! This entire activity can be done in an empty bathtub for much easier cleanup.

Special Occasions

Baby Is the Star

Materials

Video camera
Blank Tape

Activity

Create a special-occasion video of your baby and you. Choose a special holiday and begin a tradition in the first year of your baby's life. On that special day, have someone videotape you and your baby at various times. This might include waking up, meal times, or playing outside. Capture the ordinary moments along with the special ones that the day brings. In your baby's first year of life, come up with an opening line that can serve throughout the years. It might be something like, "This is the life and times of Joanna Levin. Today is February 2, 1995, and Joanna is just about to begin her day." Make sure you and the baby are in the video together. Store the video in a special box. As your baby becomes older she can help you decorate it. Each year add to the tape for a videolog of your baby's life.

What Did Baby Say?

When baby is grown, it will be fun for her to hear how she first sounded.

Materials

Tape recorder

Activity

Baby sounds are special sounds. They change from day to day. Capture the sounds by placing the tape recorder in the same room as your baby. As you turn the tape recorder on say, "It is October 11, 1995, and this is Helena Levin." Record the very early sounds of your baby crying. As your baby starts to gurgle, laugh, and giggle, tape those sounds—always remembering to begin with the date. When your baby becomes an adult, this will make a wonderful gift for a special birthday.

Special Occasions

Holiday Lights

Many holidays use candles or lights. Let baby enjoy them.

Materials

Holiday lights or candles that are lit
Stroller

Activity

December holidays use lights or candles to set the mood. Christmas lights twinkle in some homes, and Hannukah candles burn in others. Give your baby an opportunity to experience the lights.

Begin with a tour of your own home, and then extend this to a neighborhood walk. Since this has to be an evening activity, make sure baby is dressed warmly. It is also important that he is in a position that he can see lights. If you sit him in his stroller, make sure the lights are in his line of vision. Then, as you stroll, describe the various lights and candles. This is a tradition in our family, and it has made holidays a little more special. Even if we are on vacation, we find a street full of lights, park the car, and appreciate the display.

Special Songs

Create holiday magic with music

Materials

Songs that relate to holidays (See page 78 for suggestions.)

Activity

Make the holidays a special time for your baby by bringing new music into his life. From your first holiday with your baby, try singing some songs to him. It is fun to hold your baby and sing. If it is the first time you have celebrated Thanksgiving, try, "We Gather Together." If it is the Fourth of July, sing, "It's a Grand Old Flag." Any holiday song will do, but choose one that you enjoy. Your baby is not a critic and won't care if you can sing or not. He will, however, take great delight in listening to you.

Special Occasions

Play Blanket

Keep this for those special times when baby needs a change of pace.

Materials
Baby blanket
Rattles, balls, dolls, or other easily portable toys
Small tote bag

Activity
Collect all the materials and pack them away into the tote bag. Don't even think of using this bag until you go visiting. When you get to your destination, find a spot to set up your baby's play blanket. Make sure baby is comfortable with her new surroundings. Then, bring out the toys, although not all at once. She'll enjoy playing with items she doesn't see every day. She may even be willing to play by herself for a few minutes so you can visit!

When you leave, everything goes back into the bag. At home, put it away immediately. It will make you feel better knowing it is all ready for your next visit.

Boxes and Bows

Make use of the stuff that's left over.

Materials
Bows with sticky backs
Large boxes
Wrapping paper

Activity
After packages are unwrapped, let your baby play with wrappings and boxes. If the boxes are large enough, let him climb in them. With smaller boxes, give him the chance to stack and knock them down again.

Make wrapping paper balls and toss them for play. Crumpling the paper may be just as much fun for baby as throwing it. Make sure to supervise your baby and not let him eat the wrappings while playing. While a little baby will be too young for this activity, you can place a bow with a sticky back on his head and snap a picture as a remembrance of the day.

74

Bibliography of Resources

These books may serve as a resource for you when trying to find out more about your baby. Try your local bookstore and your public library.

Allison, Christine. *I'll Tell You a Story. I'll Sing You a Song.* Dell, 1987.

Astin, Althina. *How to Play with Your Baby.* North Carolina: East Woods Press, 1983.

Blaustone, Jan. *The Joy of Parenthood.* Simon and Schuster, 1993.

Brazelton, T. Berry, M.D. *Infants and Mothers.* New York: Delacorte Press. Lawrence, 1983.

Brazelton, T. Berry, M.D. *Touchpoints.* New York: Addison Wesley, 1992.

Caplan, Theresa. *The First Twelve Months of Life.* Putnam, 1993.

Fisher, John, J. (Ed.). *Johnson and Johnson—from Baby to Toddler.* Putnam, 1988.

Jessel, Camilla. *From Birth to Three.* New York: Bantam Doubleday Dell, 1990.

Keister, Edward Jr. & Sally Valente Kiester. *Better Homes and Gardens Your Baby's First Steps (3–18 months).* Iowa: Meredith Corp., 1987.

Kelly, Marguerite & Elia Parsons. *The Mother's Alamanc.* New York: Doubleday, 1975. (Revised, 1993)

Leach, Penelope. *Your Baby and Child, from Birth to Age 5.* Dorling Kindersley, Inc., 1989.

Ludington-Hoe, Dr. Susan. *How to Have a Smarter Baby.* New York: Bantam, 1985.

Marzollo, Jean. *Fathers & Babies.* New York: HarperCollins, 1993.

Ormerod, Jan. *101 Things to Do with a Baby.* New York: Mulberry Books, 1984.

Riverside Mother's Group. *Don't Forget the Rubber Ducky.*

Silver, Susan. *Baby's Best.* Simon and Schuster, 1995.

Spock, Dr. Benjamin, M.D., & Michael Rothenberg, M.D. *Dr. Spock's Baby and Child Care.* Simon and Schuster, 1992.

White, Burton. *First Three Years of Life.* Simon and Schuster, 1995.

Bibliography of Books

The books listed on this page are for you to look at and read to your baby. Do not be surprised or discouraged if your baby is more interested in chewing the pages, especially on boardbooks, or just turning pages. He or she is still interacting with a book.

Ahlberg, Janet, & Allan Ahlberg. *Peek-a-Boo!* Puffin, 1981.

Asch, Frank. *Baby in the Box.* Holiday, 1985.

Brown, Margaret Wise. *Baby Animals.* Random, 1989.

dePaola, Tomie (illustrator). *Tomie dePaola's Mother Goose.* Putnam, 1987.

Hague, Michael (illustrator). *Teddy Bear, Teddy Bear: A Classic Action Rhyme.* Morrow, 1993.

Hill, Eric. Spot. Puffin, 1988. In the same series: *Where's Spot?* and *Spot Goes to the Beach.*

Oxenbury, Helen. *I Can.* Candlwick Press, 1985. In the same series: *I Hear I See.*

Oxenbury, Helen. *Tickle, Tickle.* Macmillan, 1987. In the same series: *All Fall Down, Clap Hands,* and *Say Goodnight.*

Pragoff, Fiona. *Baby Days.* Little Simon, 1994. In the same series: *Baby Plays, Baby Says, Baby Ways.*

Sharon, Lois, & Bram, Staff. *Sharon, Lois, and Bram's Mother Goose: Songs, Finger Rhymes, Tickling Verses, Games, and More.* Little, 1986.

Slier, Debby (Photos selected by). *What Do Babies Do?* Random, 1985.

Wright, Blanche Fisher (illustrator). *Real Mother Goose.* Checkerboard.

Zelinsky, Paul O. (adapted by). *The Wheels on the Bus.* Dutton, 1990.

Bibliography of Music

CDs and Tapes

Almost every recording on CD can be found on tape, although not as readily.

Bartels, Joanie. *Lullaby Magic*. BMG Music. No date.

Berstein's Favorites. (CD) *Children's Classics*. Sony, 1991.

Bissette, Mimi. *Lullabies of Broadway*. (CD) Music for Little People, 1990.

Disney (Almost all Disney music is appropriate. Here are some of our family favorites.)

Beauty and the Beast, Soundtrack. (CD)

Classic Disney. (Cassette)

My First Sing-Along, Favorite Nursery Rhymes. (Cassette)

Snow White and the Seven Dwarfs, Soundtrack. (CD)

The Little Mermaid, Soundtrack. (CD)

Feinstein, Michael. *Pure Imagination*. (CD) Elektra, 1992.

Judy Collins Sings Baby's Morningtime. (Cassette) BMG Music, 1993.

Lewis, Shari. *Lambchop Sing-Along*. (CD) A & M, 1988.

Palmer, Hap. *Baby Song*. (This is an old record. It was the favorite in our house. It is worth begging or borrowing it from someone who might have it tucked away.)

Peter, Paul, & Mary. *Peter, Paul, and Mommy, Too*. (CD) Werner, 1993.

Raffi. *Baby Beluga*. (CD) Troubadour Records, 1982.

Raffi. *Bananaphone*. (CD) Troubadour Records, 1994.

Raffi. *Rise and Shine*. (CD) Troubadour Records, 1982.

Sharon, Lois, and Bram. (Cassette) *The Elephant Show*. Drive Entertainment, 1994.

Songs of Parenthood. (CD) Music for Little People, 1995.

The World Sings Goodnight. (CD) Silverwave, 1993.

Wee Sing-Sing Along. (Cassette) Price Stern Sloan, 1990. (This is one in an excellent series. Song books come with them.)